What Did We Do?

Before the Internet

by Samantha S. Bell

FOCUS
READERS.
BEACON

www.focusreaders.com

Focus Readers is distributed by North Star Editions:
sales@northstareditions.com | 888-417-0195

Produced for Focus Readers by Red Line Editorial.

Photographs ©: SvedOliver/Shutterstock Images, cover (left), 1 (left); Chinnapong/Shutterstock Images, cover (right), 1 (right); Nature1000/Shutterstock Images, 4; RnDmS/Shutterstock Images, 6; George Marks/iStockphoto, 8; AP Images, 10, 29; Andrey_Popov/Shutterstock Images, 12; AtnoYdur/iStockphoto, 14–15; Everett Collection/Shutterstock Images, 16; Vyntage Visuals/Shutterstock Images, 19; Rawpixel.com/Shutterstock Images, 21; Boyko.Pictures/Shutterstock Images, 23; Pra Chid/Shutterstock Images, 24; Atstock Productions/Shutterstock Images, 27

Library of Congress Cataloging-in-Publication Data
Library of Congress Cataloging-in-Publication Data is available on the Library of Congress website.

ISBN
978-1-64493-047-2 (hardcover)
978-1-64493-126-4 (paperback)
978-1-64493-284-1 (ebook pdf)
978-1-64493-205-6 (hosted ebook)

Printed in the United States of America
Mankato, MN
012020

About the Author

Samantha S. Bell is a children's writer and illustrator. She has written more than 100 nonfiction books for children. She uses the internet to find information quickly, but she still checks out books from her local library.

Table of Contents

Chapter 1

Sale Day

In 1966, Jill was 10 years old. Her family was moving to a new city. Their kitchen table was too big for their new home. They planned to sell it. They had other items to sell, too. So, they held a rummage sale.

 Today, rummage sales are often called yard sales or garage sales.

Before the internet, pinning signs to bulletin boards was one way to tell people about events.

They gathered items they wanted to sell. They put a sticker on each one to show the price.

On the day of the sale, they set up tables in their yard. They put the items out on the tables. Jill made signs. Each sign told the time and address of the sale. Jill put one at the end of her street.

People stopped by Jill's home to shop. They paid for items with cash. Jill's mom gave them change with money she got from the bank. She wrote what was sold in a notebook.

Of course, people still have sales today. But many people find it easier to buy and sell items online. Websites such as Craigslist and Amazon are popular choices.

Chapter 2

Without Websites

Today, websites make many tasks faster and easier. One example is shopping. People can look up the items a store sells. They can also place orders. Before, people had other ways to buy and sell things.

Before stores had websites, they sold more items to customers in person.

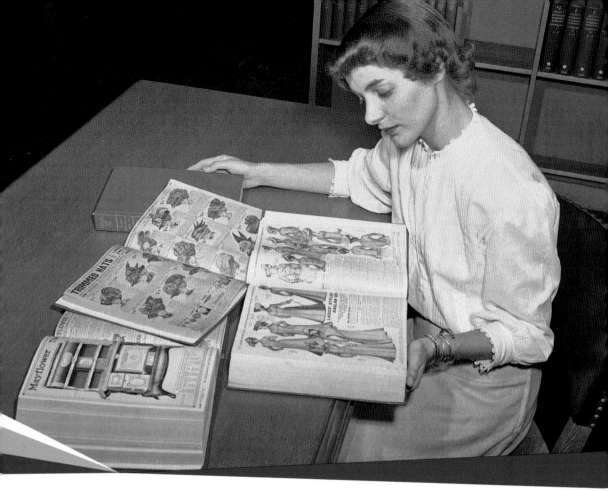

 Before the internet, more people used catalogs to order items in the mail.

In many cases, people had to go to a store in person. It was harder to buy things made far from where they lived.

Managing money is also easier with the internet. Today, many banks have websites. Users can view their **accounts** online.

Before the internet, people used more paper. Bills and **statements** came in the mail. People also sent their payments in the mail. They could send cash or write checks.

> For many years, people had to bring checks to the bank to deposit them.

Or, people could make a phone call. They told the company their credit card number. Of course, people can still do these things today. But it's often easier to pay online.

The internet also changed the way that people find information. For example, many people use **reference** books to look up facts. Examples include dictionaries and encyclopedias. In the past, people had to find a copy and look for the word or topic they wanted. Now, many people use **digital** versions. They can do a quick search with a computer or smartphone. But they must be careful. Not everything posted online is accurate.

Phone Books

Today, people can look up information about stores and businesses online. In the past, they often made phone calls instead. People used phone books to find what number to call.

Phone books have two sections. One part has white pages. This part lists people's names and home phone numbers. The other part has yellow pages. It lists businesses and their phone numbers.

Phone books are updated every year. Workers deliver the new versions to people's homes. That way, people have the correct numbers.

Phone books group businesses by category.

Chapter 3

Making Media

Today, people find a huge variety of things to play or listen to online. Thousands of people post pictures and videos. They also share music and writing. In the past, people's choices were more limited.

 Before the internet, friends often shared their favorite magazines.

Before the internet, most writing was printed. That meant writers had to find a company to **publish** their work. For many years, a few large companies made and sold most books. Other companies made magazines or newspapers. They picked the stories and pictures that

Fun Fact

Many newspapers print comic strips in each issue. The first comic strips appeared in newspapers in the 1890s.

 A printing press stamps ink onto pages for books, magazines, or newspapers.

got printed. And people had to buy or borrow copies to read them.

Many writers still publish their work in print. But it is no longer the only option. Now, people can also choose to post their writing online.

People all over the world can see it. They can share it with friends.

The internet makes sharing music easier, too. Before, musicians had to have companies record their songs. These companies sent the music to stores and radio stations.

After the 1930s, most radio stations played a certain style of music. People tuned in to find new bands and songs. But some areas didn't get many radio stations. People there had fewer options.

 Some people collected and shared records of songs they liked.

Friends could still share music with one another. But they had to use **physical** copies. Friends often traded **records** or **cassette tapes**.

The internet also changed what people could watch. Before, people mostly watched programs on TV. Companies made and **broadcast** the shows. Most TV shows played at certain times of day. If people missed a show, they could not go back and watch it. And if shows

Fun Fact

A TV network is a company that sends shows to many stations. Until the 1980s, three networks made most of the shows viewers in the United States watched.

TV BROADCASTING

1. A TV station films the show.

2. The TV station broadcasts the show as a digital signal or as radio waves.

3. The waves or signals travel through the air or by satellite.

4. An antenna, cable, or other device brings the waves or signals into a viewer's home.

5. The show appears on the screen of the viewer's TV.

played at the same time, they had to choose. People still watch TV today. But many people view shows online. They can choose when and what they want to watch.

Chapter 4

Open to Everyone

The internet changed how people find and share information. Now, websites make updates quickly. They can correct facts or make changes. In addition, more people have ways to share their work.

 Millions of people around the world create and view posts on the internet.

They use websites such as YouTube. Posting is often easy and free.

The internet also changed how people **interact**. In the past, people usually made friends with others who lived nearby. But thanks to the internet, people from all around the world can interact online.

Fun Fact

The first YouTube video was made by Jawed Karim in 2005. He called it "Me at the Zoo."

 Today, many people film, edit, and post their own videos.

Besides sharing posts, they can use comments to share ideas.

Sometimes, millions of people view a post. It spreads far in a short time. The person who made it can become famous. In fact, posting online can be a career.

Before the Internet

Write your answers on a separate piece of paper.

1. Write a sentence describing the main idea of Chapter 3.

2. Do you prefer watching shows online or on TV? Why?

3. What is one way people made payments before the internet existed?

    A. in the mail

    B. on a website

    C. with a smartphone

4. What is one reason the internet helps more people share their work?

    A. Posting online is less expensive.

    B. Posting online takes longer.

    C. Posting online reaches fewer people.

5. What does **updated** mean in this book?

*Phone books are **updated** every year. Workers deliver the new versions to people's homes.*

    A. paid for
    B. changed or made better
    C. kept the same

6. What does **options** mean in this book?

*But some areas didn't get many radio stations. People there had fewer **options**.*

    A. ideas
    B. choices
    C. amounts of money

Answer key on page 32.

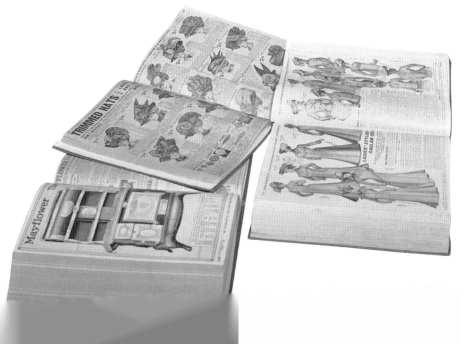

Glossary

accounts
Records of the amounts of money kept in a bank.

broadcast
Sent out radio or TV signals.

cassette tapes
Small cases holding magnetic tape that can be used to record or play sounds.

digital
Having to do with information used on a computer.

interact
To talk or spend time with another person.

physical
Related to things that can be touched or held.

publish
To print writing in a book or other format for others to read.

records
Flat disks that use tiny grooves to play sounds.

reference
Used for finding general information.

statements
Reports made by banks showing all the money that has gone into or out of an account during a certain period of time.

To Learn More

BOOKS

Kenney, Karen Latchana. *Make and Upload Your Own Videos.* Minneapolis: Lerner Publications, 2018.

Macken, JoAnn Early. *Take a Closer Look at the Internet.* South Egremont, MA: Red Chair Press, 2016.

Smibert, Angie. *The Internet.* Lake Elmo, MN: Focus Readers, 2018.

NOTE TO EDUCATORS

Visit **www.focusreaders.com** to find lesson plans, activities, links, and other resources related to this title.

Index

B
banks, 7, 11

M
mail, 11
money, 7, 11
music, 17, 20–21

P
payment, 7, 11–12
phone calls, 12, 14
posting, 13, 17, 19, 26–27

R
reference books, 13
rummage sale, 5–7

S
smartphones, 13
stores, 9–10, 14, 20

T
TV shows, 22–23

V
videos, 17, 26

W
websites, 7, 9, 11, 25–26
writing, 7, 11, 17–19

Y
YouTube, 26